In the Name of (
Merciful the Most

G000272182

DIVINE EXISTENCE VERSUS DOUBT

**Shaykh
Muhammad M. Al-Sha'rawi**

DAR AL TAQWA LTD.

© Dar Al Taqwa Ltd. 1999

ISBN 1 87 0582 26 8

Translation: Aisha Bewley

Editor: Abdalhaqq Bewley

Production: Bookwork, Norwich

Published by:
    Dar Al Taqwa Ltd.
    7A Melcombe Street
    Baker Street
    London NW1 6AE
    email : dar.altaqwa@btinternet.com

Printed and bound by:
    De-Luxe Printers
    245a Acton Lane
    London NW10 7NR
    website: http://www.de-luxe.com
    email:printers@de-luxe.com

Table of Contents

Preface

We are delighted to provide a preface to this book written by Muhammad Mitwalli ash-Sha'rani which clarifies and explains the topic of Divine Existence. The author provides us with an excellent semantic explanation of the meaning of "Praise be to Allah", Whose blessings are beyond number and are constantly overflowing without any limit. In spite of the advances which have been made in the means and methods of computation, we are still unable to calculate the outward and inward blessings with which we have been endowed. If we spent the entire length of our lives devoting ourselves to giving thanks, that would still not be adequate gratitude for Allah's blessings to us. Praise be to Allah and thanks be to Him.

When Shaykh ash-Sha'rani discusses the meaning of Divine Existence, he clearly states that it precedes the discovery of any evidence for it and that it is beyond the capacity of any human mind to fully comprehend. Allah Almighty exists in the minds of all humanity, which indicates that He existed before humanity existed and before there was any language to articulate the fact of His existence. Doubt about Allah's Existence is in reality an affirmation of it, since those who attempt to formulate evidence against it are, by doing so, in fact affirming it.

We could go on at length about this matter which the Shaykh has explained so well in these pages. We should study what he says in order to understand the matter better so that our hearts may abide in true belief in our journey through this fleeting life and possess unswerving belief in eternity and bliss in the shelter of the mercy of the All-Merciful, All-Compassionate. He is the Lord of the Immense Throne.

Part One

On *"Praise belongs to Allah, the Lord of the Worlds"*

In the name of Allah, the Merciful, the Compassionate.

Praise belongs to Allah, the Lord of the worlds.

I ask for blessings and peace on the best of Your creation and the best of Your Messengers to the worlds, our master Muhammad and all his Companions.

Foreword

"If you were to try to number Allah's blessings, you could never count them" (16:18)

There are numerous reasons for praising something. We may praise a thing for itself, but it may also contain qualities which in turn merit praise and so we also praise a thing for its qualities. When we see something beautiful, like a splendid pearl, we praise its purity, or we may praise the beauty of a lovely flower. Praise can also be given on account of blessings received or, to be more precise, for the blessings which Allah has bestowed on us. When someone is good to you, you praise him for being good. When he gives you something, you praise him for his gift. Another cause of praise is when there is a desire to obtain something from someone. You may hope to obtain something good from a person and so you praise him on that account.

Praise can also spring from fear of the threat of punishment. If I do something wrong and there is someone who is entitled to punish me immediately but who prefers mercy to punishment, then I praise him because he has done this. These are some of the elements which can form the basis of praise.

In the case of Allah Almighty, we find that He possesses all the qualities referred to above for which praise is deserved. The blessings of Allah Almighty are beyond number. He gives, opens closed doors, makes paths in this world easy to follow, bestows wealth and health, grants us success in our work, and allots His blessing to us howsoever He wishes. In all this He gives without taking anything in return. He does not need anything from us. No one can increase or diminish Allah in any way. Allah has a treasury which can never be exhausted and no one can count the blessings of Allah or number them. Allah Almighty says:

"If you were to try to number Allah's blessings, you could never count them." (16:18)

Despite all the advances in computation no one is able, or even attempts, to calculate the blessings of Allah Almighty. Allah is He whose blessings cannot be counted or numbered. If we wanted to praise Him, we could never give Him His due even if we spent the whole of our lives doing nothing but giving thanks and praise.

Praising Allah is mandatory for every believer

Allah possesses mercy for the entire universe. He designated that thankfulness to Him should be expressed in a phrase which contains only two words in Arabic: *al-hamdu lillah* – "Praise belongs to Allah". The extraordinary thing about this is that you may continue, for hours, to thank and praise a human being for one blessing he gives you and yet it may be that none of this satisfies him. But for Allah – glory be to Him and may He be exalted and His power and immensity magnified – these two words are sufficient: *al-hamdu lillah*. Thus He teaches us the extent of power and the extent of thankfulness. Allah is the One whose blessings cannot be counted or enumerated in this world or the Next. He is the One who has prepared an excellent reward for us in the Next World and a good life in this world. What He gives us is beyond what any human being in the world can give and indeed is beyond the power of all mankind together. Yet it is enough for us to utter these two words: *"Al-hamdu lillah."*

Allah, the One who gives without reckoning and bestows blessings on all His creatures, is content with these two words of thankfulness. That is why *al-hamdu lillah* comes in the *Fatiha* of the Book and also comes at the end in the words of Allah Almighty:

"The end of their call is: 'Praise be to Allah, the Lord of all the worlds!'" (10:10) Praise occurs in this world and the Next World, during the earthly lives of creatures and after all matters have returned to Allah Almighty.

It is difficult for the human intellect to ascertain an appropriate way to praise the Divine Perfection. However much eloquence and power human beings have, they will never be able to fulfil the right owed to Allah. That is why, at the beginning of His Book, Allah Almighty taught us the best way to praise Him. The form of praise is the same for all creation because that which is desired for each of the servants of Allah is to praise Him for His blessings. Not all the servants of Allah would be equally able to formulate an appropriate form with which to praise Allah.

When Allah teaches us to praise Him with the words *al-hamdu lillah* He imposes the same obligation on all His servants whether they are educated or illiterate. So Allah's teaching His servants the form of giving praise is yet another blessing for which Allah deserves praise. That is why, therefore, when a man wants to praise Allah for His blessings, He must also praise Him for teaching him the way to give praise and so he continues constantly praising and Allah Almighty continues to be constantly praised.

Even before Allah Almighty placed words of praise on our lips, He created blessings for us which deserved our praise. When we examine the order of things, we find that Allah's blessings to man preceded man's existence. Allah created the heavens and the earth and determined its nourishment and provision. When man was brought into existence by the word "Be!" all these blessings already existed.

Adam was the father of all humanity when Allah Almighty created him. He lived in a Garden in which he experienced no tiredness or unhappiness and had everything he needed for his life. Adam was a man without a past – he came to life without having a precedent history – but the blessings of Allah Almighty were there before him and were waiting for him to provide him with everything he needed for a wholesome life. He did not create anything for himself. Allah Almighty created it all for him.

7

This preceded any human capacity to praise Allah. It was a prior state which demands that we must say *"Al-hamdu lillah"* out of gratitude for the blessings which Allah has bestowed on us .

Chapter One
Divine Existence and Phenomenal Existence

Allah and Being

When we discuss Allah Almighty and His connection to phenomenal existence, we find that there are many who try to counter this with scepticism or denial and make great efforts to present misguiding evidence in support of their opinions.

Before beginning this discussion, I would like to state that the thinking of such self-deluded and self-destructive people shows complete lack of understanding of Allah's *deen* and can only be voiced by those who disobey Allah and will do anything to cast doubt on the existence of Allah. This signifies a person who is inwardly disobedient towards Allah and this disobedience renders him sleepless. He has an innate consciousness that there will be a Final Reckoning and an Afterlife and that he will meet Allah; and his denial of it makes him try to raise doubts about the *deen*. It may even be that he actually deludes himself about there being no Reckoning or Punishment.

Philosophers have striven for many years to propagate scepticism about the Divine Religions and they have devoted their intellects to that end. Other philosophers have held that *deen* denotes slavery and that 'freedom' means freedom from religion. These theorists postulate an erroneous assertion.

Belief in Allah also stimulates people to exert themselves. Each person tries to formulate a viewpoint in support of his position and all the debate continues without end. The very activity of the inquiry into the evidence for the existence of a supernatural metaphysical power; or into evidence to negate its existence means that we in fact have an innate natural capacity to recognise Allah and that there exists inside ourselves something which affirms that Allah exists. Otherwise the human soul would not exhaust its energy in trying to resolve this debate and the human mind would be happy and care-free with outward knowledge of the material world which Allah created for it.

But when we look at the materialists we see inside them a terrible anxiety which robs them of sleep and makes them anxious despite their material success. We find the highest incidence of insanity and suicide in the nations which are the most advanced materially. That is because a man may achieve material success, which many people may envy if they look only at the life of this world, but nevertheless he lives in terrible anxiety because his soul is not in harmony with existence. A soul can only be in harmony with existence by having belief in Allah and following His Path.

"He is the Living the Self-Sustaining..."

We read in the noble *ayat* in which every believer takes refuge – the Throne Verse:

> *"Allah There is no god but Him, the Living, the All-Sustaining. He is not subject to drowsiness or sleep. Everything in the heavens and the earth belongs to Him. Who can intercede with Him except by His permission? He knows what is before them and behind them but they cannot grasp any of His knowledge save what He wills. His Footstool encompasses the heavens and the earth and their preservation does not tire Him. He is the Most High, the Magnificent."* (2:255)

He is the Living who is everlastingly alive; death does not touch Him because He created both life and death. He is the All-Sustaining who looks after His Kingdom. This requires explanation. Some people believe that Allah created existence, set up His laws in it and then left it to run according to the laws which He set in motion. These are precise laws which are not disturbed by time or affected by anything. However, Allah Almighty wants to inform us that He created existence, set up laws in it but also oversees it continually. Allah Almighty attends to His Kingdom and never neglects it for a single instant.

What do these words mean? They mean that in His existence Allah Almighty tells us that we should never despair. Why? Because Allah Almighty set up the laws of existence and told us to make use of the means He has created and to follow these laws. But when we find ourselves powerless before these laws and have made use of the all means at our disposal without attaining our goal, the All-Sustaining who attends to His kingdom is always there. He can open the door to anything and achieve things which we consider to be impossible.

Man cries out, "O Lord!" because of his faith that He is Allah Almighty Who is in constant control of his existence, He Who gives the Truth victory over the false and defends the wronged against the wronger. So when man seeks refuge with Allah Almighty, he knows that Allah has the power to help him when all other means have been exhausted. When he has made use of all the secondary means at hand and has received no response, he still knows that Allah Almighty is attending to His kingdom at every instant and can transform hardship into ease and despair into hope and joy.

Hajar, peace be upon her, left her child at the well of Zamzam and went to seek water but her efforts proved unfruitful. After running to and fro seven times she became exhausted and despair touched her heart. Then her child, a weak infant who had no control over any of the means of this world at all, struck the earth with his foot and water gushed forth.

The Messenger of Allah, may Allah bless him and grant him peace, made use of secondary means when calling people to Islam, such as when he went to Ta'if from Makka and experienced abuse from the foolish children there. Then Allah took His Messenger on the Night Journey to confirm him and he doubled his efforts in

11

calling people to Islam, both the people of Makka and those delegations which came there during the *hajj*. At tht point a delegation came from Madina and gave allegiance to the Messenger of Allah and that was the beginning of the *Hijra* and the spread of Islam.

If each person were to examine his life, he would find that he has passed through times in which all his normal means were blocked and he was seized by overwhelming despair, finding no solution to the problem confronting him. Then suddenly the solution came unexpectedly out of the blue. Allah Almighty looks after His Kingdom. When the believer despairs, he seeks refuge in Allah and feels at peace and tranquillity because he knows that Allah hears and sees and looks after His Kingdom, never abandoning it for a single instant.

"He is not subject to drowsiness or sleep"

The Throne Verse continues by saying, *"He is not subject to drowsiness or sleep"*, meaning "He never sleeps and is never heedless." By saying this, Allah desires to calm those souls that are beset by anxiety arising from the cares of the world. He wants to restore their peace of mind and security. Therefore He reassures them by saying, *"He is not subject to drowsiness or sleep,"* meaning that He is never unaware of anything, even for an instant. So this believing soul is at peace because it knows that Allah is not heedless of what the wrongdoers do.

This soul sleeps peacefully at night. Why? Because Allah Almighty does not sleep. He tells the person who believes: "You may sleep and need fear nothing. I do not sleep. I guard you while you are asleep and while you are awake. So do not let anxiety overcome you to the extent of thinking that your enemies are going to attack you while you are asleep, constantly fretting so that you go to bed with apprehension filling your heart. I am Allah. I do not sleep. I know and witness everything, so rest content with Me and My protection."

A man sleeps peacefully when he puts a guard, sentry or watchman at the door of his house who does not sleep during the night.

So how much more should that be the case for someone who knows that Allah is guarding him? How great is his feeling of security when he knows that the Power which created this existence and brought it into being is protecting him? Therefore a true believer feels constantly at peace with Allah and secure in the knowledge of Allah's taking care of him even in his darkest moments and harshest times.

The noble *ayat* continues to stress how the human soul can be in harmony with the rest of existence which Allah has created. Allah says: *"Everything in the heavens and the earth belongs to Him."* This increases the equanimity of the human soul. Allah Almighty tells His servant, "What are you afraid of? That sustenance will not reach you tomorrow? That you will not complete a task you have to do tomorrow? That the money you need will not arrive tomorrow? Remember that everything in the heavens and the earth is My property which I give to whomever I wish and withhold from whomever I wish. What is the source of your anxiety when I am the One who controls and gives? What are you thinking about when I can give you what you want because all that you see before you and much more which you do not see belongs to Me? From it I give whatever I wish to whomever I wish."

"Beware of fearing the morrow or being apprehensive and feeling that you are alone in this world. I am with you. I am the Living who does not die. I exist eternally and never sleep and I do not overlook anything. Everything in the heavens and the earth is under My control. As long as you are My slave and believe in Me, be untroubled regarding My decree. If I provide for those who reject Me and ask you to veil those who disobey Me, how much more will the provision be for someone who obeys me and believes in Me?"

The noble *ayat* continues: *"Who can intercede with Him except by His permission?"* Allah wants to affirm to us that He alone gives intercession to the one He permits, meaning: "Do not fear any person in this world, no matter how unjust. Do not fear anyone, however great a tyrant. None of these people can intercede with Me so that I will give them power over you. But the one who can intercede with Me is the one to whom I give permission.

Whoever has permission from Allah must be near to Allah. Every wrongdoer and tyrant in the earth is far from Allah."

Chapter Two
Allah is the King and the Giver

Allah Almighty desires to increase the faith and tranquillity of the heart of those who worship Him. Therefore He tells them, *"He knows what is before them and behind them. But they cannot grasp any of His knowledge save what He wills."* In other words: "Do not imagine that I do not know what happens and what is planned for you. I know what is before you, i.e. what you divulge publicly, and what is behind you, i.e. what you conceal and hide, because I am aware of your actions, your intentions, and what your hearts conceal. So you should not fear that I will miss anything or that any of My creation will be hidden from Me, even what is in people's hearts which they do not divulge to anyone."

Allah Almighty says: *"He knows your secrets and what is even more concealed."* (20:7) This means that Allah knows every secret. What is a secret? A secret is something, knowledge of which is shared between two people alone, something I resolve to do and then confide to one of my friends or relatives. That is a secret. *"What is even more concealed"* is something which is hidden in the heart and not divulged to anyone. So a matter which remains in someone's breast, about which he never speaks and never confides to anyone, is not hidden from Allah Almighty. Allah is aware of it. Since this is the case, what are you afraid of? Allah knows everything. Since Allah does not sleep, why are you afraid to go to sleep?

The gifts of Allah are manifold

Then Allah Almighty says, *"But they cannot grasp any of His knowledge save what He wills."* This means that Allah disseminates His knowledge in different ways.

• Knowledge which He gives to whomever He wishes of His servants.

• Knowledge which he gives to all mankind.

• Knowledge particular to Allah Himself which He does not give to any of His servants.

The knowledge which Allah gives to whomever He wishes of His servants is that which Allah gave to His Messengers and His righteous friends. This is an unveiling which Allah grants to whomever He wishes among His servants. It is not possible to speak about it because it is a gift specific to an individual and it is not a general subject of debate.

As for the knowledge which Allah gives to all mankind, it is the material knowledge which Allah unveils to mankind generation after generation. Every part of this knowledge emerges at the time which Allah has predetermined for it. When the emergence of this knowledge coincides with a man or people investigating and striving to reach it, Allah Almighty gives it to them. When this knowledge does not coincide with people who are searching for it, Allah gives it to mankind by what is called 'chance' or 'coincidence'.

For instance, it may happen that someone is doing research about something and then discovers something completely different to what he was looking for. This discovery is unrelated to the research he is doing. That which comes about through coincidence is an unveiling from Allah because the appropriate time for the emergence of that knowledge to mankind has come. That is why we often hear of a scholar who is involved in a particular line of research who suddenly, in the course of his work, encounters an unexpected discovery which he did not expect to find. We say that this is chance but in reality it was simply the time for that knowledge to be made known to mankind. It comes into existence from the knowledge of Allah to the knowledge of mankind by the word "Be!" because the time has come for that knowledge which was stipulated from pre-eternity.

As for the knowledge of Allah Almighty which is particular to Himself, no human being can attain to it. This is the general meaning of the *ayat*. Whatever the knowledge of those who lie in wait for you, whatever they have prepared, Allah is the One who truly knows. His knowledge is above their knowledge. He knows what will nullify their knowledge and render it powerless. All of this is so that the believing heart will feel at peace with the Decree of Allah and so that all believers will know that they are safe and secure as long as Allah Almighty is caring for them and guarding them.

The gift of Lordship

Before continuing with this discussion, I would like to explain an important point. Allah Almighty possesses both the gift of Lordship and the gift of Divinity. Allah Almighty is the Lord of the worlds. He bestows the gift of Lordship on all, as He informs us when He says:

> "When your Lord took out all their descendants from the loins of the children of Adam and made them testify against themselves: 'Am I not your Lord?' They said, 'We testify that indeed You are!'" (7:172)

Why did Allah not say, "Am I not your God?" and so have them testify to His Divinity? It was because the gift referred to here is the gift of the Lordship of Allah, the Lord of the worlds. What then is the gift of Lordship? The gift of Lordship is a gift equally distributed amongst all of Allah's creation. Allah bestows the gift of Lordship on all He has created. For instance, Allah

Almighty created existence and made it subject to man. Existence contains many forces which are more immense and more powerful than man but they have been subjected to him by the judgement of Allah who has made them subservient to him. The sun, earth and winds and many awesome forces in the universe are much greater than man.

The sun is potentially able to burn up the earth and all those on it. If the earth were to cease revolving, all of mankind would be destroyed. The winds are able destroy life, and water to drown people. When the rains stop, the rivers dry up and life ceases. All of these forces and many others which Allah has created in balance in existence are forces more powerful than man and greater than him, but they have been put to the service of man.

The sun cannot say. "I will shine today and be absent tomorrow." Water does not inundate the whole earth nor does it leave it completely desiccated. The earth cannot stop revolving by its own volition. But all these things represent awesome powers which have been subjected to the service of man by the will of Allah. They have no volition of their own and cannot disobey Allah at all.

In His bestowal of these powers Allah is manifesting the gift of Lordship and in doing so He does not distinguish between believer and unbeliever. He gives these things to all of His creation. The sun shines for both the believer and the unbeliever. The earth is cultivated by those who believe and those who do not believe. The rain falls on believing communities and on people who do not worship Allah.

The laws of the earth are the gift of Lordship. Those who cultivate the earth well and take care of it obtain an ample harvest whether they are believers or not. Those who neglect their land and do not cultivate it do not obtain any harvest from it, whatever their belief. Those who profit from the knowledge of Allah which Allah has disclosed to humanity by generating new industries in the world will pluck the fruit of their action.

Thus in the gift of Lordship Allah does not distinguish between one man and another and the laws which Allah sets out in the earth and the means which Allah mentions when He made His creation testify to Him and, He asked, *"Am I not your Lord?"*

The gift of Divinity

The gift of Divinity, on the other hand, is a gift restricted to those who believe that there is no god but Allah. Belief here is a contract between man and his Lord. That is the reason why the Noble Qur'an begins *Surat al-Baqara* with the words of the Almighty:

"ALIF. LAM. MIM. That is the Book with no doubt. In it is guidance for the godfearing: those who believe in the Unseen and establish the prayer and give of what We have provided for them; who believe in what has been sent down to you and what was sent down before you, and are certain of the Next World. They are the people guided by their Lord. They are the successful." (2:1-5)

In His Mighty Book Allah Almighty always addresses the believers saying, *"O you who believe."* So belief in Allah Almighty is the basic condition of the gift of Divinity. It comprises belief in the Unseen, belief in the Resurrection after death and the Reckoning, and it involves following the Path to the serene life of faith which Allah has laid out in His Mighty Book for those who believe.

So the gift of Divinity entails a good life in this world and in the Next World for all who believe in Allah, do not associate anything with Him, and follow the Path which Allah has set out for us in His Book and which He has made clear to us. This Path contains the rectification of every kind of corruption which can affect our life in this world. Allah created it to bring about a just human society which is dominated by ease and security and filled with blessing.

The gift of Divinity entails tranquillity for the heart

Most of the laws by which we are governed today are the result of legislation by fallible human beings and yet we then express

19

astonishment at the misery existing in the society which has been created by these laws. If we were to implement what Allah Almighty has stipulated in His Mighty Book this would most certainly not be the case, for there we have a perfect blueprint to enable mankind to develop a virtuous society. That is because of the difference between the extremely limited capacity of the human being and the unlimited knowledge of Allah Almighty. Allah created the human soul and He created existence. He knows best what will help the human being and what is best for him in his life.

That is why the believers who follow the Path of Allah feel the gift of Divinity inside their hearts which are thereby filled with tranquillity. When the noble *ayat* was revealed to the Messenger of Allah, may Allah bless him and grant him peace, *"Allah will protect you from people"* (5:67), the Messenger of Allah dismissed those Companions who used to surround him to defend him when the unbelievers or hypocrites tried to harm him. Why? Because Allah Almighty is the greatest Power who created everything. He was guarding him and so he had no need of a human guard. No human being could approach him or injure him if Allah was his protector.

'Umar ibn al-Khattab used to sleep in the shade of a tree without any guard. Why? Because his heart was filled with the noble *ayat*: *"He is not subject to drowsiness or sleep."* Therefore he used to sleep at peace alone in the shade of a tree, believing that Allah Almighty, the One who does not sleep, is stronger and more powerful than anyone else who might guard him. He is stronger and more powerful than any guard in this world. That is why he slept under the tree in Allah's protection. No one was able to come near him and so he was safe and at peace.

Chapter Three
Faith

Faith is something which you have or do not have. The meaning of belief in Allah is that you believe and confirm that there is a Great Power which is disconnected from every whim and desire. It is that Power which created this universe and subjected it to you. There is nothing like this Power in respect of knowledge, creation, mercy, vengeance, and all the attributes of Allah Almighty. So when faith enters the heart, we must not compare our knowledge to the Knowledge of Allah nor our power to the Power of Allah Almighty.

When Allah Almighty says, "Act," I am not entitled to ask "Why?" There can be no argument except between two equals – and what a difference there is between the Power of Allah and the power of a human being! When He says, "Do not do it," I am not entitled to say "Why?" because the Knowledge of Allah cannot be compared to my knowledge. In spite of that, we find some people who argue without shame and claim to be qualified to quarrel with the Knowledge of Allah and to argue with Allah about the Path of Life He has laid out for people to follow.

Faith in Allah Almighty means surrendering to the Power of Allah, above which there is no power, and to the Knowledge of Allah, above which there is no knowledge. There is nothing like Allah Almighty. This is the sign of the entry of faith into the human soul. It is an entry which only comes after reflection and pondering over existence and its indications, even though some people call it slavehood. They say that the *Deen* is slavehood. We say, "Yes, the *Deen* is slavehood to Allah Almighty but there is a great difference between being a slave to Allah and being a slave

21

to mankind. When a human being enslaves you, he wants to take from you or utilise your capacity to increase his capacity and to deprive you of the blessing which you can obtain and add it to the blessing which he controls and owns. When a man enslaves a group of people, he makes them work for his sake and they culti-vate the land while he takes its crops; they care for the buildings while he owns them. So the slavehood of mankind entails stripping the slave of every good which he might achieve for his own bene-fit. Slavehood to Allah is a very different matter.

What is slavehood to Allah?

Slavehood to Allah is a slavehood which increases your power, gives you good, blessing, and increase from the gift of Allah Almighty to you for your best interests. Allah Almighty is rich beyond need of anything in existence. He has no need of your energy, your property or anything you possess in this world. Allah Almighty is the Master of everything. All property is in reality Allah's property. It moves from hand to hand and each man only takes his provision from it. Allah Almighty says:

"Men have a portion of what they acquire" (4:32)

In this *ayat* Allah explains the profound wisdom that the provi-sion which you acquire or earn is not yours alone. Your wife has a portion, your children have a portion, and a number of Allah's creatures have a portion in it. We are sometimes amazed by a miser who does not enjoy the provision Allah has given him and we ask ourselves in wonder, "Why does he do that?" We may even criticise what he does. The answer to that is that this wealth which he earns and for which he is avid is not in fact his provision but rather the provision of other creatures. He is merely a custodian of it until he conveys it to them. So he cannot spend it or enjoy it. Provision remains like that without being touched until it reaches the one whose provision it actually is.

Slavehood to Allah Almighty is a gift from Allah to His slaves. Allah possesses the Kingdom of the heavens and the earth. He does not want us to worship Him in order to make use of our energy, obtain the fruits of our labour, or gain anything whatsoever. He is the One who provides for us and gives to us in every instance. He bestows on us and blesses us in our endeavours. He is the One who makes every difficult thing easy for us and opens locked doors for us.

Slavehood to Allah Almighty is only for our improvement. It increases the slave in everything, gives him blessing in his property, health and children, and preserves him from every evil and harm. Slavehood to another human being is something else. In human slavehood the master exploits the effort, toil and sweat of another man for his own benefit. What a difference there is between the two!

Allah Almighty has promised His believing slaves a good life. So when He tells me to do something, He desires nothing for Himself but merely intends my happiness in this world and the Next World by it because my action will not increase the Kingdom of Allah in any way and my not doing something will not decrease it. One of the consequences of faith is that when I follow the Path of Allah, I choose the good life which is not dependent on my power, but rather dependent on the Power of Allah Almighty with Whom nothing can compare. One of the consequences of lack of faith is that I debate, philosophise and decide according to my limited capacity. The difference between faith and lack of faith is the choice between the life which Allah has ordained by His unlimited and boundless Power and by His Knowledge which cannot be attained by man, and a life which I sketch out with my limited intellect in conformity with the capricious whims and desires which pervade my soul.

O people, let us ponder existence!

In all of His Divine Messages Allah Almighty asks us to ponder existence and to study the Signs of Allah. Why did Allah command us to do this? If there had been any evidence at all in existence which indicated lack of unity or power on Allah's part, Allah would not have commanded us to reflect on it or to contemplate ourselves, because if someone shows you something with a flaw in it, he does not tell you to examine it thoroughly. On the contrary, he uses various means to distract you from the thing which you are looking at so that you do not discern the flaws or faults in it. If someone tells you to contemplate, reflect and examine something he must be certain of its perfection.

I will give a simple example which is easy to grasp. When you go to buy anything in this world and the owner or maker of that thing comes to you, one of two things applies. If the article is perfect and splendid its craftsman will tell you to examine it well. When you have examined it once, he will tell you to look at it again and then again. This is so that you will be able to discern the fineness of the craftsmanship and recognise the perfection of the item. But if an item has faults of any kind then its maker tries to trick and deceive you. He uses all manner of tricks to divert your attention from what is in your hand so that you do not discern its flaws and imperfections.

In His Noble Qur'an Allah Almighty asks us to contemplate creation and to ponder existence. He tells us that there are clear Signs in existence. There are clear Signs in ourselves and in the creation of the heaven of the earth. The Almighty says:

"We will show them Our Signs on the horizon and within themselves until it is clear to them that it is the truth."

(41:53)

The Challenge

If the One who uttered these words were not the Creator of existence and the Creator of mankind and the Knower of the secrets of everything, would He not fear that there might be faults, imperfections and things which He did not know that might produce a contrary result? But Allah Almighty is the Creator. He is

24

the One who speaks and He is the Knower. He knows the minute details of everything He has created. That is why He says, "Ponder creation. Examine it and you will find My Signs; you will see the powerlessness of My creation and the omnipotence of My Power. Look inside yourselves and the result will be the same." Allah stresses:

"We will show them Our Signs on the horizon and within themselves until it is clear to them that it is the truth."

(41:53)

He is the One who placed Signs and miracles in existence which indicate His immensity and power. When we ponder it, we discern the immensity of Allah Almighty, and this is the primary purpose of the human intellect. The purpose of contemplation of existence is to enable recognition of what Allah has created. Man will only be in harmony when He humbles himself to his Creator.

"We offered the Trust to the heavens, the earth and the mountains but they refused to take it on and shrank from it. But man took it on. He is indeed wrongdoing and igno-rant." (33:72)

What is the Trust (*al-Amana*)?

What is the Trust? "The Trust" in this context refers to freedom of choice without any external pressure. Allah describes man as being "ignorant" when he agreed to accept this trust, meaning that he neglected to recognise and assess the responsibility and weight it involved. We will offer a small example which will make this easier to grasp. Suppose that a man comes to me and gives me some money and says, "I am entrusting you with this." Then he comes every month, or at regular intervals, to give me another amount and says, "I am entrusting you with this." Then I take this property and enjoy myself with it and waste it. Then the time of reckoning comes when the owner of the property asks for his

25

money but I have none of it left. This is what happens in this world.

Allah Almighty gives to us what cannot be counted or numbered. Then He says, "You may enjoy all of this but you have a Trust for which you are responsible: that you do not corrupt the earth, do not steal, and do not use My blessings to disobey Me or to wrong people." Man accepted the Trust but Shaytan found an opportunity to insinuate himself when man it took on. Allah said to man, "Do this," and "Do not do this," but did not place any restriction or pressure on his free will. This freedom of choice means that there can be a Reckoning for which each man will be entirely answerable.

Allah sent Divine Messages to make the Right Path clear to man but the Trust which he took on, and that which all the rest of Allah's creatures refused to carry, gave him freedom to act or not act, the freedom to oppose and disobey Allah. When Allah says, "Do this" and "Do not do this", it is within the capacity of man to obey or not to obey. Only man, of all existence, is able to do that. The mountains, for instance, have no choice, neither does the sun, moon, or stars. The sun cannot say, "I will shine during the night." The angels have no choice and they do what they are commanded.

But man, the one who took on the Trust, accepted freedom of choice in this world. What did he do with it? His ignorance gave rise to many things. He worshipped things which do not benefit or harm him: the sun, fire, stones, idols, and beasts of prey. The Creator originated this existence which He manages. Human beings began to deny the blessing of Allah and abandon the Messages which Allah revealed as a mercy to form the basis of a wholesome, safe life for human beings and human society. Man began to make his own laws and abandon the *Shari'a* of Allah. His whims overcame him. He began to base his social structures on the desires of the lower self and not the Truth. Therefore misery afflicts him in this world and disasters have occurred.

But why does man do that? Allah Almighty has summarised it with splendid eloquence. He describes the extent of how Shaytan insinuates himself into the human soul. Allah reports in the Noble Qur'an how Shaytan deluded Adam into disobeying Allah. That is

26

when he completed the delusion. In a single sentence in the Qur'an, Allah describes how Shaytan deluded man:

"Shall I show you the way to the Tree of Everlasting Life and to a kingdom which will never fade away?" (20:120)

Chapter Four
Man's Quest in this World

Man desires two things in this world: immortality and unlimited wealth. He wants to live forever and never die and to have endless wealth which will enable him to lead the life of luxury and vanity which the lower self desires. He wants his wealth to be unaffected by anything detrimental and for his age to be unaffected by the passing years. He desires eternal youth and inexhaustible treasure.

Man's earthly desires provide a secure opportunity for Shaytan to reach the human soul. All the gods which man creates and worships are either an illusion designed to bring about provision and importance in the world or an illusion designed to avert harm or illness which might lead to death – which is an end that can never be evaded. The false worship indulged in by the human soul is brought about by desire for these two things and his gods are what he hopes will realise them for him. The truth is that these 'deities' cannot bring about either goal, nor do they possess any power to benefit or harm even themselves. But the fear which Shaytan inspires in the unbelieving soul is what makes it weaken to such an extent that it believes that there is effective power in existence possessed by something other than Allah Almighty.

Whose help should be sought?

The illusion of benefit or harm coming from other than Allah appears to the human soul because of its lack of faith, but the believer knows that Allah alone has Power and that He is the One

Who defends him, protects him, cares for him and guards him, even when man sleeps, because the Eye of Allah never sleeps. Anyone suffering under the delusion is seeking the help of those who have no power except for the tiny amount which is lent to them by Allah. What a difference there is between the power of mankind and the Power of Allah! So the only sensible course is to leave our affairs to the One who is neither harmed nor helped by our lack of faith in Him. It is pure ignorance on my part which makes me resort to other than Allah. I generate this ignorance in myself and I want to realise it.

Let us further clarify this point. Say, for instance, I want to get hold of someone else's property to which I am not entitled. The life pattern which Allah has delineated tells me not to do that. It tells me this first of all to protect me. I am one individual in a society and when I consider the property of someone else to be fair game, I establish this as a principle. Then there would be millions of people in this society who would have the right to think of my property as fair game as well. So Allah Almighty has forbidden that in order to protect me. If I reflect, I will recognise that not allowing myself to take other people's property protects me and my property, but I want *"a kingdom which will never fade away."*

Allah informs me how Shaytan tempts me so that I will be able to recognise when this happens and protect myself from the slips and mistakes he suggests to me. But in spite of Allah's warning, I still allow full rein to the desire inside me to possess *'an unlimited kingdom which will never fade away'*, and so I seize other people's property. Nevertheless there is still a dormant faculty deep inside me which sees Allah and knows Him well. This is my conscience which will rob me of sleep and through which I sense the retribution awaiting me for my disobedience and abandonment of the *Shari'a* of Allah in favour of my own desires. So I do all kinds of things to try to assuage my conscience and lull the disquiet which fills my heart, makes it sleepless and oppresses it when it is immersed in disobedience to Allah.

We will give an example of that. Let us say that we bring to a young man in a bloom of his youth the most beautiful girl in the world and tell him that she is his for the night. Then we open a

29

hidden door in the room looking out onto the Fire of Hell and tell him that if he takes her he will end up there the following day. He will be most unlikely to indulge his appetite. However because the retribution is veiled from us, Shaytan comes to us trying to convince us that there will be no retribution. This illusion is what permits us to give unlimited rein to our appetites and allows us to wrong others. In trying to deny the existence of Allah and trying to sow doubt, the furthest that a disobedient soul can go is to claim that Allah does not exist. But Allah does exist and it is only the freedom which He has given us that enables us to deny Him. For this reason doubt about the existence of Allah is, in reality, affirmation of His existence.

Part Two

Divine Existence versus Doubt

Chapter One

Correct Beliefs

Islam is either founded on correct beliefs, which is the *deen*, or without correct beliefs, which is hypocrisy. But to begin this discussion we must first define the meaning of correct beliefs (*'aqida*). Correct doctrinal beliefs are those which develop in the heart with which it is completely content and then these beliefs become certain for you to the extent that it does not occur to the intellect to argue against them. They are unassailable to study, investigation, research and argument; the heart is completely at rest in them. If the intellect finds any need to continue to argue it means that your faith is deficient. When the desert Arabs said, "We believe," what did Allah say to them?

> *"Say: 'You do not believe. Say rather, "We have become Muslim," for belief has not yet entered into your hearts.'"*
> (49:14)

So faith consists of those correct beliefs with which the heart is completely at peace and which it does not occur to the intellect to question. They do not come into the sphere of the senses or any sphere which is subject to the senses, meaning that you cannot say to someone, "I am a believer because I actually see you before me." The arena of faith is the Unseen, something invisible to you which you cannot see and which is unattainable to your senses.

That is why we often try to coin a metaphor for faith and say that it is being as certain as you are about something which you can actually see. We say, "I am certain that this will happen" or "I believe that will happen as surely as I see you in front of me." I cannot see that it will happen: it may or may not happen. I cannot be unequivocal about it but I affirm it by my belief and say, "This will happen as surely as I see you before me", to demonstrate my certainty about something unseen.

Since that is the case with the minor matters of this world, how much more should it be the case with belief in Allah Almighty? Certitude here should have a high degree. In the words of the *hadith* you should worship Allah as if you could see Him, for though you do not see Him, He sees you. If faith moves into the arena of debate and mental argument, it departs from its true meaning and is no longer real faith. If there is intellectual debate about it, it means that your faith is not complete.

The debate centres on the evidence, or lack of it, for the existence of Allah. Consider first the person who argues for Allah's existence. What impels them to do that? What makes them exhaust their minds and thought to set forth evidence for the existence of Allah? What compels people to this is that Allah is innately recognised by every human being in their natural form. Those who believe in Him obey Him and implement His teachings. But those who are prodigal against themselves and yet are aware of the immensity of the punishment which awaits them have an intuitive feeling by which they naturally recognise Allah but they exert their minds to try to attack the *deen* of Allah. What they are really doing is trying to flee intellectually, by any means they can devise, from the final Reckoning which awaits them.

A person who attempts to set out evidence either for the existence or the non-existence of Allah actually affirms His Existence without any need for evidence. Evidence for the existence of Allah lies in the very fact of the quest for it, because the quest and the mind's effort in pursuing it is only possible because knowledge of Allah exists in us naturally and we are aware of and sense His existence and recognise that He exists.

Divine existence is prior to any evidence for it

The existence of Allah precedes any evidence for it; and the attempt to prove it, which will continue until this life ends, is in reality a proclamation that Allah exists. We attempt to use evidence suitable to our intellects. If we investigate and closely examine the Divine Messages which Allah has sent to us we will find that the greatest and most direct proofs are those which are formulated by that method which is most appropriate for the human intellect and its past and present capacities, and the details of it fill a person with a sense of complete powerlessness.

When we examine the knowledge of Allah and how it reaches man, we find that it occurs through the connection of words to the intellect as Allah Almighty shows us by His Words:

"He taught Adam all the names." (2:31)

This means that Allah Almighty taught Adam the meanings and names of everything in existence. Then Allah brought the angels and said to them, *"Inform me of the names of these."* They did not know and said, *"Glory be to Allah. We have no knowledge except what You have taught us."*

Thus the concept or thing must exist first and be recognised by the listener and already exist in his mind before there is a word to make that concept known to the intellect. For instance, when we say the word 'house', it already has a specific meaning in our minds. It is a place where people live which is made from stone or other materials. So when the word is mentioned, the idea which already exists in the intellect emerges and is accepted.

On the other hand, when you utter a word which has no meaning for a particular person, their intellect does not understand it and does not recognise its existence. An example of this is if you were to approach a man who lives on flat land and has never seen or heard of a mountain and say "mountain" to him, he would not have any conception of what the word "mountain" means and would therefore not understand it. He would not understand it or recognise it because it has not entered his mind before. Similarly, if you tell a man that something is done by computer, he will not be able to understand what you mean if he does not know what a computer does.

But when you say "Allah", all intellects understand what you mean: that overwhelming powerful Force which created the universe. But we have never seen Allah, so how can we understand this word? If knowledge of Allah did not exist in us in our natural form and did not already exist in our intellects and souls, we would never be able to understand and accept this universal concept which is in harmony with the human soul. It is our certainty of the existence of Allah which enables us to understand this word.

The knowledge of Allah's existence, found naturally in us, is what gives the concept access to our minds because no word can be understood unless its significance and meaning already exist in the human mind. The existence of a concept must precede the word which describes it. You cannot say a word like 'mountain' or 'strong' to someone and expect him to understand what you are saying unless the concept already exists in his mind before you articulate the word. Therefore the meaning must exist before words which indicate it can come into being and be understood.

If we consult dictionaries for any language anywhere in the world, we will find that all the words in them apply to things which already exist. These dictionaries are reviewed every year to add words that have come into existence during the previous year, showing that the existence of a thing necessarily precedes the name it is subsequently given. There are many words added to dictionaries every year and there are specialist scholars who have meetings about language in which they devise names for new ideas or things which have not existed before. So the rule is that a thing exists first and then man gives it a name.

The fact that the name "God" exists in all languages of the earth and always has done signifies that Allah Almighty must have existed before the existence of mankind itself and before man spoke in any language.

The existence of Allah is beyond the capacity of the human intellect to comprehend

The expression "God" has a single meaning in all minds and all languages. The human intellect accepts the name "God", therefore showing that human beings recognise the concept of Divinity naturally, even though it is beyond the capacity of the human intellect to comprehend exactly what it means. In this context we refer again to the noble *ayat* which says:

> *"When your Lord took out all their descendants from the loins of the children of Adam and made them testify against themselves: 'Am I not your Lord?' They said, 'We testify that indeed You are!' Lest you say on the Day of Rising, 'We were heedless of this.'"* (7:172)

This noble *ayat* from Allah indicates to us how knowledge of Allah exists in us intuitively despite the fact that it is beyond the capacity of the intellect to grasp. We know, with certitude, that Allah exists. This recognition exists inside us even if no one directs us to it. So when the name of Allah is mentioned, we do not feel that a person is uttering some strange and meaningless expression. We understand His Strength and Power and that life is only harmonious because He exists.

There are illiterate people who cannot read or write. Perhaps they have never read a single word in their entire lives. If you tell them about something in this world they have never heard of they ask you what you are talking about and say "We do not understand you." The one exception to this is the word "God". If you say it, both the ignorant and the scholar, the young and the old, everyone who hears you knows what it means.

The reason for this is that knowledge of Allah exists within us innately in our natural form. So the child worships Him. The simple man who has never read a single word in his entire life worships Him. The educated man worships Him. The man who is well-versed in knowledge and has obtained the highest degree worships Him. In spite of their disparate levels of knowledge, all these intellects which may be unable to reach a shared understanding about any other matter, experience no conflict where Allah is concerned.

If you enter a mosque, you will find all Allah's servants sitting together, so different in age, education, social standing, character, custom and everything else, but in harmony regarding the worship of Allah. They bow to Him together, prostrate to Him together, recite the Qur'an together, and glorify Him together. All of these intellects could not be joined and be harmonious if we did not have some innate capacity by which we know Allah, as is confirmed the noble *ayat* quoted above.

Chapter Two

Doubt is Affirmation of Divine Existence

In the case of those who try to deny the existence of Allah, the attempt at denial is itself in reality a kind of affirmation because there is no need to deny something which does not exist. For instance, some people say that the earth is round while others say that it is flat. There is a debate. If people did not see the earth stretching out flat in front of them and if science had not told them that the earth was round, the debate would not have occurred. There is a debate about this matter because scientific fact differs from what the eye actually sees. So it consists of denial and debate because both possibilities exist. If we want to deny a scientific theory, the theory must first exist. Otherwise how could it be denied?

In the same way the attempt to deny the existence of Allah is necessarily preceded by the fact that Allah does actually exist. Otherwise why would any unbeliever try to deny it? The attempt at denial and debate can only occur around something that exists. When there is no basis for the existence of a thing, there is no possibility of arguing about it. If something does not exist in the first place what is the existence which is being denied? Doubt about the existence of Allah is then affirmation of His existence and so those who try to formulate proofs to create doubt about the existence of Allah are in reality affirming His existence. As has been illustrated, evidence for the existence of Allah is in itself evidence of His existence.

So we have reached this truth, which is that knowledge of Allah exists in us innately in our natural form, and every human heart and soul consciously or unconsciously knows this, so that those who disbelieve in Allah still fear Him and fear the Day of Reckoning but are trying to deny it. They are trying to deny the punishment which awaits them and to convince themselves that this punishment will not happen and will not take place, even though they have to lie to themselves to do it. The attempt at denial arises out of the fear of meeting Allah and terror at the prospect of what threatens them in the face of their refusal to acknowledge the reality.

It is an attempt to still their trembling souls inwardly and allay what they sense about the Day of Reckoning. It is an attempt to calm their souls by deluding themselves into believing that there will be no Reckoning. They concentrate on piling up evidence to persuade themselves of the non-existence of Allah, even though they know at the bottom of their hearts that it is false. This ensures that the unbelieving soul remains in misery in this world until it reaches its term and never knows true peace of mind. It always fears tomorrow even if it somehow manages to assuage its anxiety today.

The Path of Allah entails restricting human passions

If the Path of Allah is so clear and so advantageous why do so many people abandon it? Why, when the Path of Allah entails justice and happiness for all people, does the human soul try to select another path for itself? Sometimes humanity is provoked by contemporary thought and modern theories but more often the reason for denial has nothing to do with the intellect but is due to the fact that Allah Almighty places restrictions on the whims and desires of the human self. These restrictions are not established for the welfare of a specific group but for the welfare of all mankind.

Human avarice, however, is boundless and man wants to give his passions free rein, even though he knows that this will entail great harm to society. There is, for instance, the love of possession. Man wants to own everything – great piles of gold and silver – more than they would be able to spend, even if they lived many lives. Nor will they be able to take it with them when they die.

40

Since that is impossible, why are there wars over ownership? The answer is that the human soul, despite the certainty of death, thinks that its life will go on indefinitely. That is why the Messenger of Allah, may Allah bless him and grant him peace said:

> "I have not seen any certainty more likely to be doubted than the certainty of death."

But Allah Almighty encourages us to discipline the desire to possess and forbids infringement against the property of others in order to protect every individual in society and so that everyone in society respects the rights of everyone else. He forbids unlawful possession of property and usurping the rights of the weak, thus protecting them from the aggression of the strong. He forbids the consumption of the property of orphans who are unable to protect themselves. He forbids theft so that the strong may protect the weak and the strong may be protected from the strong.

Allah is the One who has forbidden me to take the property of someone else just as He has forbidden others, who make up the rest of society, to take my property. So He protects society from me but at the same time protects me from society. However strong I am as an individual, I am much weaker than society as a whole. If Allah permitted me to consume the property of the weak, He would, by the same token, permit all society to take my property without let or hindrance.

The justice of Allah is to protect the weak from the strong and at the same time, the strong are also protected from society. So this legislation is in the best interests of all society, the wealthy and poor, the weak and strong. Allah has also encouraged mercy, affection and brotherhood so that the rich will give some of their property to the poor, so that society will enjoy peace, and so that rancour, enmity, and hatred will leave people's hearts and be replaced by compassion for other people.

This, therefore, is one of the laws of Allah Almighty. He is clearly opposed to the avarice of some human beings who desire to possess without limit, appropriate the rights of others without hindrance, and generally to tyrannise others, so He established limits to protect people from themselves and from their desires which could lead them to destruction in this world and the Next, and to protect human society as a whole.

When we move from the acquisitive to the sexual appetite, we find that in this area Allah Almighty has also protected the individual human being from what will corrupt them and has also protected society as a whole. It is related that a man came to the Messenger of Allah, may Allah bless him and grant him peace, and said, "I will take the contract of Islam with you, but I am a man who loves women and I cannot leave this habit. What do you permit me?"

The Messenger of Allah did not beat him, throttle him or send him to be stoned. He acted as a teacher who wanted to clarify the wisdom of the law regarding this matter. He wanted to make it clear to him in a way that he would truly understand it. He calmly asked, "Would you like someone to do that with your mother?" Anger showed on the man's face and he said, "No." The Messenger of Allah asked, "Would you like someone to do that with your wife?" The man quickly replied, "No, no." The Messenger of Allah, may Allah bless him and grant him peace said to him, "All of us are like that, brother of the Arabs."

This made it clear to him that the legislation of Allah is established to protect his mother, sister and wife from what would be unacceptable to any man. If any individual remembers this conversation while intending to commit fornication, then he will remember that he would hate his mother, sister or wife to do it and will immediately abandon what he intended to do. So legislation in this instance limits the appetites and places restrictions on them. Allah established these limits in order to protect the individual himself by protecting his mother, sister and wife from any violation thus defending his honour. Man is happy with that. But while being happy with legislation to protect his own family from any violation from society, it does not necessarily prevent him from violating the family of someone else.

Some people want a personal law which allows them to steal while preventing others from doing so, where it is lawful for them to violate other people's honour but unlawful that their honour should be violated. They want to spy and disclose the defects of others and to speak badly of them, but when someone spies on their defects or speaks badly about them, they become enraged.

Allah says: "No, all of you are equal before me. You are My slaves, I created you and deal with all of you without distinction. I do not allow one person what I forbid to another, even if it is a ruler with power. When I make something unlawful, I make it unlawful for all of you. When I make something lawful, I make it lawful for all of you, strong and weak, poor and rich. Whoever reckons that his property, rank or power make him special with me is deluded."

This is Divine justice. This is the Path of Allah which does not differentiate between anyone. It does not allow one person and forbid another the same thing. Its legislation aims to protect all of society, rich and poor, strong and weak.

The Wisdom of the Path of Allah

Allah has laid out the rules for a strong, healthy society. He rectifies the human soul and builds it from within and makes it firm, strong and just, so that people are as keen to preserve the rights of others as they are to preserve their own rights. He eliminates the law of the jungle which prevails between animals and raises man to a high level of humanity by which he is distinguished from the rest of His creatures.

Allah Almighty has set out this path for us for the establishment of a just society to rule the earth. He is higher than all mankind and knows more than they do. He is the One who created existence and subjected everything in it to the service of man, and so the sun, moon, earth and all the stars serve man. Allah Almighty created all these powers and made them subservient to man. They are powers beyond anything man is able to create. Man cannot create earth, heaven, the sun or moon, the atmosphere or the force of gravity.

Allah alone is able to set out for us the correct course for a happy life on this earth. Man, however strong he is, has no right to become insolent and claim that he is better able than Allah Almighty to define the sound Path. This is because no matter how advanced we consider ourselves, are still powerless in face of the Power of Allah. All of us, however much we try and desire to be just and balanced, still have desires and appetites in us while Allah has no desires. That is why He judges with justice and sets out the Straight Path. Allah knows more than all of us put together which is why we must follow the Path of Allah and not rely on any human system, whatever it is.

Who created life?

Many people accept the existence of Allah so the question must be asked why do they not then follow the Path of Allah? We find that some of them cannot answer this while others try to replace the Path of Allah with a human course counter to it and then to justify the path they have taken. Such people contradict themselves. If Allah is the Creator of life and the Creator of existence and has established a course for human life in the same way that He established all the laws of existence, how can you abandon this gift and accept instead what a human being says out of his own whims and desires? How can you leave the One who knows and resort to someone who does not know? How can you argue against what the Creator has established in favour of what a creature has brought into being?

The basis for following the Path of Allah is belief. That is why we find that Allah Almighty addresses His servants by always saying, "O you who believe." He repeats it in many *ayats* of the Qur'an because the basis of following the Path of Allah is belief in Allah and His Messenger, the angels and the Unseen. Any other basis is false. If you do what Allah asks of you without belief, your actions are useless.

In clarification of this we might take the example of *sadaqa* which Allah has commanded us to give to the poor. Whoever does so, seeking the pleasure of Allah and with belief in Allah will have the promised reward. But if someone gives *sadaqa* to people so that it might be said of him that he is generous, or if someone gives *sadaqa* publicly but when a poor person comes to his house when he is on his own, he drives him away and does not give him *sadaqa*, showing that his intention in giving is reputation and fame, not Allah's pleasure, they are not rewarded even though they are performing an action which Allah Almighty has encouraged and asks us to perform. Such people do so while their hearts do not believe in Allah. They are not in conformity with the words of Allah Almighty, "O you who believe". Similarly if a man prays in front of people but does not pray when alone, is he rewarded for his prayer? Never, if he does what Allah commanded without faith.

Allah Almighty has no need of associates. When an action is for the Sake of Allah and His pleasure, He accepts it. When it is to please people, He has no need of it and does not accept it. If a portion of it is for the sake of pleasing people or for the standing in this world, He does not accept it either. Allah is rich beyond need of the worlds. The noble *hadith* says:

"Actions are according to intentions, and every man has what he intends."

This noble *hadith* is the clearest elucidation of the matter. The intention is located in the heart. Allah Almighty is aware of people's hearts and knows everything they conceal with complete knowledge. However, some people in this world believe that they can deceive Allah. This is a total delusion.

45

Chapter Three

The Efforts of Philosophers to Prove Divine Existence

Philosophers have striven over the course of centuries to adduce the existence of Allah, attempting to use the intellect rather than the Divine Messages which Allah Almighty revealed to teach mankind about Himself. They have tried to use the intellect for something for which it was not created. The intellect has several vital functions but adducing the existence of Allah is not one of them because that is beyond its capacity. It does not use the means or the Messages which Allah revealed to His slaves. These are the Messages in which Allah has provided evidence which is within the capacity of the human intellect from the day He created it until the Day of Rising, but the philosophers wanted to go beyond this by applying the human intellect to something beyond its capacity.

Allah Almighty tells man in His Messages how to worship and know Him. He explained it to us and made the reward for doing so and the punishment for not doing so clear to us. This is at the same time strong evidence for the existence of the Creator because those who worship the sun, idols and anything other than Allah, do not receive any messages from them. Their false gods do not explain existence to them or teach them the way to worship. That is why we do not hear of any messenger sent by the sun to guide people, although people worship the sun. We do not hear of a messenger sent by any idol to guide people although people worship idols, stones, animals, and many other things which people themselves have innovated according to their own whims and desires.

Logic and the intellect with regard to metaphysical realities

When we are ruled by logic and intellect, neither of them require us to involve ourselves in things which are beyond their capacity. It is pure ignorance which makes man attempt to pierce the veils of those mighty matters which the intellect cannot comprehend. So we do not find any school of philosophy which manages to pierce the veils of metaphysical realities or the Unseen worlds. They reach the same impasse which other schools have reached before them. The results of each school contradict the others and none of them reach a result which all intellects accept.

Man's connection to the outside world takes place through what we call the senses or sense perception so that when you, as a human being, connect to the world which surrounds you, you do so by means of your hearing, sight, smell, touch and taste. It is by means of these senses that we understand the world, that we give it the attributes by which we describe it. The attributes of colour, for instance, are distinguished by sight; the attributes of flavour, defined by the words sweet, bitter, delicious, and foul, are experienced through our sense of taste, and so forth.

So we connect to the outside world by means of these senses; but what about the world which is inside the human soul? What is the nature of the connection between a human being and what is inside him? Is it possible for a human being to have a complete connection with what exists inside him? Is this connection achieved by the senses or by means of other faculties which some people call intuition and others call inspiration? Some people use other terms for it but what is certain is that the connection to what is inside the human soul is not achieved by means of the five senses by which it connects to the outside world, but by other means which are described as inspiration, intuition, gut feeling and other things.

We will expand on this subject by giving some further details. We will begin first with the things of the outer world which man has access to by means of his senses, so he sees different colours, hears different sounds, touches different textures, tastes different flavours and smells different scents. This is man's connection to the outside world. His connection to what is inside of him comes, on the other hand, by means of his feelings which he applies to other things like love and hate. For instance, a man loves one person and hates another or certain things without there being any known sensory cause for such preferences.

The senses, inner perception and the existence of Allah

There are things inside of us which allow us to be aware of specific feelings. We are aware of these feelings and recognise them completely but we do not perceive them through our senses. Man, however much he may seek to explain the causes of love and hate, cannot discover the sense which feels the love or hatred. This sense is not one of the five senses by which the human being is connected to the outside world, or which define man's connection to it. When scholars study the senses they are eager to say, "These senses are what connect man to the outside world and man has faculties, instincts, feelings, inspiration and other things inside of him which connect him to the inside of the human soul and affect it."

People who deny logic can state that there are no faculties inside of man other than the senses which connect him to the outside world but the truth is that inspiration, feeling, or sensation of what is inside the human soul, exists before the human self is even aware of the world around it. That is the *sunna* of creation. A small child is aware of hunger and thirst and expresses them by crying before he can use his senses to connect to the outside world. He feels tenderness, warmth, love, hate, cruelty and mercy. All these things exist inside him within seconds of being born. It takes weeks or months for the outer senses to fulfil their task in a way which the child can fully comprehend.

When we study these internal sensations we find that their faculties derive from man's sensitivity to the existence of Allah

Almighty. This sensitivity needs further definition in respect of the immensity and power of Allah, and His being and existence and other details, but nevertheless it confirms the existence of a faculty inside of man by which he is aware of and senses the existence of his Creator.

So the meaning of the name of Allah, for instance, cannot be grasped by the five senses because it is beyond their scope but an inner faculty of man does grasp it. It is an invisible kind of perception. The reality of the word "God" is beyond the scope of the five senses, yet we find that when the ear hears it, it understands it. We have already explained that it is fundamentally impossible for the ear to understand anything which does not already exist within the human soul. In the case of the word "God", however, the concept is not unfamiliar to the soul. It is known to it in a way which we do not understand and cannot analyse. When someone mentions the name "Allah" to us, that which immediately leaps to mind is the existence of an extraordinary Power which created this universe, even if this power is outside the scope of the intellect and the scope of the senses.

Do we perceive the existence of Divine Power?

So how do we grasp the existence of this Divine Power? How can its name be familiar to us? It is beyond the scope of the senses and outside the scope of the intellect. It is something inside the soul: inspiration or awareness. It tells us that this Power exists, despite the fact that it is beyond the grasp of the intellect and senses. Awareness of it must already exist inside the soul for the soul to able to grasp it.

Philosophy began in ancient times, particularly among the ancient Greeks, to study metaphysics and look beyond the physical world, and to study the Force which brought this world into existence. Who told them that there was something beyond the physical world to be studied? How did they know that there was something different from matter, even though the five senses only convey information about material existence. We are not debating

Greek philosophy or whether this or any other philosophy succeeds or fails. It is a subject which does not concern us here. What concerns us is that these ancient philosophers were impelled to study the metaphysical and the fact that there were things inside themselves which were not sensory nor subject to the senses.

Since the dawn of time man has studied the metaphysical by various means, sometimes using it as another way to manifest his humility or slavehood to a Power which is beyond the physical. But the important thing in all of this is that there are inner feelings within the human soul which tell it that there is something beyond empirical nature, that there is a Power beyond this world, and that this Power is an immense and extraordinary Force. In other words, there is an inner feeling of the existence of Allah in every human soul. The Force which is beyond this existence conveys something to the human soul that makes it grasp or understand that there must be an extraordinary and powerful ordering Force beyond the material world which people see.

But the material world itself in which we live cannot create these feelings in us. There is no way for the five senses to perceive that there is a powerful overwhelming Power behind all of this. So there must be another force apart from this material world which places that concept in us. Our knowledge that there is something other than physical matter which must be the object of examination. Thus examination, thought and turning towards this Power begins. If there were no feelings and strong awareness of the existence of this Power inside us, we would never have thought of investigating it and this investigation would not have entered into the history of mankind.

Chapter Four

Reflection on the Divine Existence

Another observation which I want to make is that when man reaches a stage when he can reflect on the existence of Allah or a stage in which he understands that there is a Power beyond this existence, part of his life must have already passed. Most people do not begin to reflect about or discuss such matters in depth until they are twenty or thirty years of age, when they have sufficient intellectual maturity to debate such a profound matter. The question which should be posed here is: by what logic did those people worship Allah before reaching this age? How did they understand all of this philosophy which requires a mature intellect, knowledge and study?

Yet we find that simple intellects which have not read a single book or studied this subject know that Allah exists and worship Him with understanding. We find that those who do not debate this subject at all accept the existence of Allah and worship Him without feeling that there is any contradiction between the existence in which they live and the existence of the Almighty Creator.

The passions of the human self

Why do some people try to prove the existence of Allah while others deny it altogether? What is the reason for this extraordinary contradiction which exists in spite of the fact that, as we have seen, the human self naturally innately that which affirms the existence of Allah? This dichotomy occurs because of the whims and desires of the lower self. All those who try to delve into this subject use imagination rather than logic and prejudice rather than reflection.

I want to give an example here to clarify that. If we lock the door of a room where we are sitting and then someone knocks on it, all of us know that something is knocking on the door. This is our common perception and is the point on which there is no disagreement. Then we begin to ask ourselves who is knocking on the door? A man or a woman? Short or tall? White or black? Arab or non-Arab? Here the dispute begins because we start relying not on logic and intellect, but on imagination.

This is what happens to people who try to comprehend Allah when to do so is beyond the scope of the human intellect and an impossibility. That is because the imagined thing must resemble something which is within the capacity of the intellect to formulate. If you want to explain a particular thing to someone who has not seen it, you do so in the terms of something with which he is already familiar, or he will not be able to grasp what you are talking about. However, nothing is like Allah Almighty.

All that the philosophers say about Him is based on conceptual thinking. The intellect cannot perceive Him and He is not subject to logic. Indeed, there is no point in applying logic to the subject, because Allah Almighty Himself tells us all that we can know of Him and how to worship. Yet we want to exceed that and touch on things which are not within the scope of the human intellect. Sound logic in fact dictates that we should hold to what Allah tells us.

Confirmation of the existence of Allah exists in our hearts naturally and the path of worship of Allah and how to obey Him and all that He wants us to know about Him exists in His Messages which He sent by means of His chosen Prophets. So logic tells us that we should follow these Messages and it is imagination which tells us that we should investigate what is beyond the scope of the intellect, despite the fact that the Messages of Allah to mankind truly contain the greatest linguistic evidence of the existence of Allah.

The Signs of Allah on earth are numerous

Now I want to point out an important statement in the noble *ayat*:

"We will show them Our Signs on the horizons and within themselves until it is clear to them that it is the truth." (41:53)

Why did Allah not say: "We will show them Our Signs on earth?" Instead He used the word "horizons". We know that the Qur'an, which is the Word of Allah Almighty, is extremely precise, and the choice of expression is completely appropriate to the intended meaning. Allah Almighty wants to call our attention to the fact that in the future He will disclose to us Signs on the horizons which we do not yet know. Man's reaching the moon, the attempt to reach Mars and all the attempts to discover the secrets of existence on the horizons surrounding the earth confirm this noble *ayat*, but some people are deluded by science, forgetting that this knowledge has come to mankind by the power of Allah Almighty.

Some people try to philosophise about the expressions of the Qur'an, trying to reduce them to the limited scope of the human intellect. Orientalists, for instance, try to create doubt about the Noble Qur'an. They say, for instance, that Allah Almighty says: *"Both East and West belong to Allah, so wherever you turn, there is the Face of Allah."* (2:115) and then commands us to direct ourselves to the *qibla* in our prayers, to the extent that the prayer becomes invalid if we do not face *qibla*. Since this *ayat* makes it clear that Allah Almighty is in every place, both the east and the west, whatever direction you turn, they say that this is inconsistent with the insistence on a specific direction towards which we must face in the prayer to Allah Almighty.

The issue here is one of faith based upon the recognition of Divinity and that the knowledge of Allah Almighty is above every knowledge, and that as long as you believe in Allah and submit to this great Force, Allah Almighty will choose the best and most correct Path for you. You follow this Path because it has come from Allah Almighty. This is faith. The intellect is not equal to it. What a difference there is between the Power of Allah Almighty and the power of human intellect! Belief in Allah is based on submission to His Divinity. This is why Allah mentions the question of the *qibla*.

The location of the *qibla* does not burden the believer at all; there are no new burdens or hardship connected to it. If the direction is to the east, or to the west, to the right or the left, none of this imposes any hardship on the believer in his prayer, and so there is no hardship when it is directed to the west instead of the east. Turning in any direction requires exactly the same amount of effort.

Another *ayat* which deserves consideration is the one in which Allah Almighty mentions the *qibla* in His Book: *"The fools among the people will ask, 'What has made them turn around from the direction they used to face?'"* (2:142) An important aspect of this *ayat* is that it uses the future tense. The future tense is only used to refer to something which is going to take place in the future. It is not possible to say, "So-and-so will do such-and-such" while he is actually doing it. It must be something he has not yet done but will do in the future.

In His Noble Book Allah says to His noble Prophet, may Allah bless him and grant him peace, *"The fools will say..."* meaning that they are going to say this but they have not said it yet. After the change of *qibla*, this will be said by those who are the enemies of the *Deen* who try to create doubts about it and spread falsehoods about it. Allah also describes those people as fools even before they speak. Then He informs His Prophet and the believers that those fools will say, *"What has made them turn around from the direction they used to face?*

This means that Allah Almighty challenges those unbelievers in a future time which has not yet arrived and tells them that they will say this and that those who do so are fools. This is a miracle. It involves a choice: they can say it or not say it. Moreover Allah Almighty described them in a derogatory manner as "fools".

54

The Qur'an is the Word of Allah by which He will be worshipped until the Day of Rising and no change or alteration will be made to it. What would happen, hypothetically, if those people heard the *ayat* and did not ask about the change of *qibla* and avoided the matter completely? They would be able to attack the Qur'an and attack the *deen* at its most vulnerable point. They could come and say that Muhammad, peace be upon him, said in the words which were revealed to him from Allah that people referred to as fools would come and ask what had turned the Muslims from their *qibla* but since no one ever had questioned this it is clear that these words were not inspired and that the *deen* is therefore from Muhammad.

But Allah Almighty is the Speaker and He is the Doer. He put in the hands of the opponents of Muhammad the possibility of showing the Message to be untrue. He says that fools among people will come and ask about the reason for the change of the *qibla* from Jerusalem to the Masjid al-Haram. "I am telling you about them before they come and what they will say before they say it." Then he announces that those people are fools. But those unbelievers actually come and do say these words, repeating exactly what the Qur'an says, and thereby affirm the truthfulness of the Words of Allah although they are in fact trying to misguide people from His *deen*. This illustrates how Allah has brought decisive evidence of the truthfulness of this Noble Book at the hands of the opponents of the Qur'an, and has made those who strive against His *Deen* actually affirm it by the command of Allah.

So the change of *qibla* embodies a great miracle of faith, for Allah Almighty issued a challenge to the opponents of this *Deen* which was well within their power to take up. His Words, *"Both East and West belong to Allah,"* also foreshow that Islam will spread in all regions of the world and that those who pray in every place will adopt different directions. One will face east towards the *qibla* while another faces west, another north and another south, even though all of them face towards a single point, the Sacred House of Allah. From all directions they face the House of Allah.

The physical *qibla* symbolises the unity of the goal of the Muslims. Facing the Sacred House of Allah is a sign of submission to Allah. For instance, the kissing of a stone and throwing of pebbles during the *Hajj* are not a question of logic or intellect but a matter of humble submission to the commands of Allah Almighty. There is a wisdom in everything which He commands you and in your response you fall into one of three categories.

Either you are a believer in Allah, in which case you will follow what Allah says by the right of His Divine Authority over you and your slavehood to Him. That is why we find that acts of obedience in the Qur'an are addressed to the believers. He does not say, "O mankind, do not this; do that," but "O you who believe..." The believer who accepts with certitude Allah's authority over him is the one who is addressed. He follows the instructions given in the same way that a sick person will follow what a great doctor tells him to do for the treatment of his illness. He accepts that the knowledge of the doctor is much greater than his own knowledge. How much more is that the case with Allah for there is no comparison between His knowledge and the knowledge of any man.

Or secondly, you are a straightforward unbeliever or rejector, in which case you will simply do whatever you want. "There is no sin at all after disbelief" because an unbeliever has torn up the instructions of the greatest Doctor and followed his own whims for treatment. No one blames him because there is no sin after disbelief. If you have no faith, do whatever you like.

Or thirdly, you may be a man who worships his intellect. Such a man wants to employ his intellect to reach a stage which is level with the knowledge of Allah Almighty. This person is misguided and wretched and will not achieve anything because no one can encompass the knowledge of Allah. Such people refuse to be encompassed by the mercy of Allah and follow their minds without achieving anything.

Allah Almighty has made faith a test of the human soul and its submission to Him. He says, "If you want to worship Me and believe in Me and acknowledge that there is no god but Me, this is the Path. Do this and do not do that. This is a test of your obedience and belief and the firmness of this belief in your heart. If you believe in me as a Lord and Creator, then worship Me in the manner I have defined for you." When I worship Allah, I worship Him as He wishes to be worshipped. I do not invent a path according to my own legislation and intellect to worship Allah. He is Allah and I am the slave.

The change of the *qibla* was a test of belief. Turning to the east or west does not require any effort from the believer. But Allah Almighty says:

> *"We only appointed the direction you used to face in order to know him who follows the Messenger from him who turns round on his heels. Though in truth it is a very hard thing — except for those Allah has guided. Allah would not let your belief go to waste. Allah is All-Gentle, Most Merciful to mankind."* (2:143)

Who argues about the issue of faith?

But those who argue about the issue of faith do not offer any proof or evidence for what they say. They avoid debating the core of the Message or the Path which Allah has set forth for His slaves. An individual may state, "This Qur'an was not revealed by Allah." This cannot be established. He did not bring his negative knowledge by any definitive means. It arises out of his desire to legitimise his own passions which necessitates fleeing from the *Shari'a* of Allah to another law which will allow him to indulge in his own whims and desires and despoil others of their rights.

We find some who say that man is descended from an ape, a thesis based entirely on supposition, for none of those who say this have any evidence whatsoever that a monkey can turn into a man. When we begin the debate, we must say to him: "Come, have you seen a monkey turn into a man?" "No," he will reply. "Did you witness the creation of man?" "No" is the reply. "Did you witness the creation of the monkey?" "No," he will again reply. "Can you turn a monkey into a human being?" "No." "Then what is the basis of your theory?"

The creation of man contains evidence of Divine Existence

The vast gap between man and other creatures is completely inexplicable in terms of the theory of natural selection and can only really be understood in terms of the Power of Allah. It is the Power of Allah Almighty which takes a handful of earth and says "Be!", and there is man, who lives on the earth, builds, prospers, and goes to the moon. Look at what mankind can do now and what they will do in the future and you will see what happens when the Power of Allah touches the handful of earth.

However, in its depths the human self is an enigma even to the person himself. There are powers within it which Allah has not disclosed to man even now. Most men never understand themselves or plumb their depths and secrets and to this day there are many aspects of human conduct which remain an enigma to researchers. There are laws that govern us which we know about but there are many other laws we do not know about at all which govern most of our behaviour. For instance, when a man loves he does not know why he loves. The person you love may not merit your affection and sometimes may even be very evil and contain qualities which you despise. But, in spite of that, you love them.

Love and hate are two emotions whose laws the human intellect does not understand. Indeed, in many cases, they contain things contrary to logic and intellect. Emotionally, the human soul is a strange mixture of logic and illogic, intellect and non-intellect, altruism and egotism. It is an enigma which still remains an enigma.

However, although the human self is an enigma which we cannot understand, it has a basic nature of which we are all aware. That nature is the connection of the soul to Allah. Allah brings the natural form into existence in us and so the child, the young person, mature person, the educated and ignorant all recognise it. They all recognise the Word of Allah and their souls tremble when they hear it despite the disparity between their intellects. That is because Allah Almighty knows them, and the happiest of souls is the soul at peace to whom Allah gives the happiness of this world and the Next, the soul which is at peace with His Word, justice, strength, power, knowledge and existence. The believer is certain that Allah is real, the Next World is real, and that this world is real, and so acts accordingly. The believer is certain that Allah will help him because he has chosen His Path and he is certain that Allah's decree is the best thing for him. What Allah gives is good and what He withholds is good. His withholding is a mercy because it preserves us from what would otherwise be bad for us. The believer knows that Allah will defend those who believe, that Allah loves His believing slaves, that He is merciful in His Decree to the believing soul, and the believer knows that there is no wrongdoer stronger than the justice of Allah, or tyrant above the Power of Allah, or corrupter who will escape the punishment of Allah.

"The end of their call is: 'Praise be to Allah, the Lord of all the worlds!'" (10:10)